THE SERENITY PRAYER

*A simple prayer
to enrich your life*

TREVOR HUDSON

MONARCH BOOKS

Oxford, UK & Grand Rapids, Michigan

First published in 2002 in South Africa by Struik Christian Books Ltd,
a division of New Holland Publishing (South Africa) (Pty) Ltd
(New Holland Publishing is a member of the
Johnnic Publishing Group)

First published in the UK by Monarch Books
(a publishing imprint of Lion Hudson plc),
Mayfield House, 256 Banbury Road, Oxford OX2 7DH
Tel: +44 (0) 1865 302750 Fax: +44 (0) 1865 302757
Email: monarch@lionhudson.com
www.lionhudson.com

UK ISBN 1 85424 656 9
US ISBN 0 8254 6069 7

Distributed by:
UK: Marston Book Services Ltd, PO Box 269,
Abingdon, Oxon OX14 4YN;
USA: Kregel Publications, PO Box 2607,
Grand Rapids, Michigan 49501.

Unless otherwise stated, all Scripture quotations are from
the Holy Bible, New International Version,
© 1973, 1978, 1984 by the International Bible Society.
All rights reserved.

British Library Cataloguing Data
A catalogue record for this book is available
from the British Library.

Book design and production for the publishers by Lion Hudson plc.
Printed in Singapore.

DEDICATION

To all recovering alcoholics at AA,
especially my close friends, whose changed lives
testify to a power greater than our own,

and

to Debbie, Joni and Mark, whose faithful
love and companionship mean more
than they will ever know.

CONTENTS

GRATITUDES

TO BILL MEAKER WHO ENCOURAGED ME to publish a small book and then helped me to write one. His support throughout the months of writing was generous, insightful and immensely helpful;

To Rhonda Crouse and Fiona Lee whose enthusiasm about the idea behind the book fuelled my desire to write it, and to Annake Müller and the rest of the team from Struik Christian Books for their part in getting the manuscript ready for publication;

To John H who read each chapter through 'AA eyes' and kept nudging me to write in a more down-to-earth, practical and simple manner;

To Schalk Pienaar for taking the time to read the manuscript and offer some helpful suggestions;

To Dallas Willard whose writings and friendship continues to shape my thinking about the way God relates to us;

To Lyn Meyer who placed at the service of this book her many typing and computer skills;

To Debbie Joubert for her help in proofreading the completed manuscript.

To my brothers and sisters in the faith at Northfield Methodist Church with whom I share my life and who constantly encourage me in my walk with God through their faithfulness and love;

And last, but certainly not least,

To Debbie, partner in marriage, and our children, Joni and Mark, who keep reminding me that there is far more to life than writing books, and without whose love and friendship I doubt whether I would write at all.

I owe you all an immense debt of gratitude and thankfulness and appreciation.

AN INVITATION TO FIND DEEPER PEACE

*A*S A PASTOR I SPEND MANY HOURS listening to people. People who are struggling in one way or another with the living of their lives. People who are finding life difficult. People who are looking for something. When I reflect on these conversations, there often seems to be a common theme running through them. Put simply, I would describe it as a search for peace.

They seldom use these exact words. They don't say, "I'm looking for peace." Their desire for peace is not something abstract or philosophical. Usually it is set in motion by some experience of struggle or pain in their everyday lives. While preparing to write this little book, I kept notes of some of the ways in which this longing for a more peaceful life disguised itself. Here are some of the things people have shared with me:

"My marriage is going well, the children are fine, I've got a stable job, but I am still restless inside. There must be more to life than getting married, having kids, and going to work. But I can't put my finger on what it is."

"I worry a lot. I think I am a born worrier. I'm always apprehensive that something is going to go wrong. Or I am going to forget to do something that I am supposed to do. Even during the night I wake up and make lists of what I need to do."

"I'm really stressed out at the moment. I've got deadlines to meet, jobs to do, people to see and I don't know how I am going to fit it all in. I need more hours in the day."

"Ever since the accident I've blamed myself for what happened. How can I get over the guilt that I feel?"

"I don't know what to do with my teenage son any more. He has become very rebellious. He won't listen to me any more. What can I do?"

"I'm frightened by what is going on around me. My neighbours were hijacked recently and I wonder when it is going to happen to me."

"My husband died last year. What's the use of going on living?"

I wonder if you can identify with some of these sentiments. They represent those everyday struggles that come to all of us at some stage of our lives. Struggles like inner discontent, anxiety, stress at work, guilt, pain in our close relationships, fear, grief. When we find ourselves struggling with issues like these, they often become sources of inner conflict and turmoil for us. We begin to wonder where we can find peace of heart and mind – with ourselves, with others and with God.

This longing for peace doesn't only take place in our personal lives. It also happens at a wider social level. Unpeace is the curse of our age. The headlines of our daily newspapers make it clear that we live in an unpeaceful world of spiralling violence, growing antagonisms between the nations, deepening divisions between rich and poor and widespread corruption in the corridors of power. Despite all the "peace initiatives", "peace talks", "peace-keeping forces", the world's need for peace cries out to the heavens.

Against this background of turmoil and conflict in both our personal and social worlds, I want to offer you a simple prayer. It is known as the Serenity Prayer. Many people, whether they are religious or not, are familiar with the shortened version of the prayer. It can be found on wall plaques, bookmarks, bumper stickers and in many inspirational writings. Countless people recovering from alcoholism and other addictions pray it daily as part of their "twelve-step" recovery programme. Even more have found that this prayer has helped them to find peace in the midst of their hurried, hassled and hectic lives. It goes like this:

> God, grant me the serenity
> to accept the things I cannot change,
> the courage to change the things I can,
> and the wisdom to know the difference.

Not so many people know that these words are part of a longer prayer. When I first came across the full prayer I was immediately taken by its spiritual wisdom, insight and depth. It seemed to convey deep truths in a very simple, accessible and practical way. When I began to use this prayer in my own devotions I found it enormously helpful. I was also struck by how helpful others found it when I shared it with them. It continues as follows:

> Living one day at a time,
> enjoying one moment at a time,
> accepting hardships as the pathway to peace,
> taking, as he did, this sinful world as it is,

not as I would have it,
trusting that he will make all things right
if I surrender to his will –
that I may be reasonably happy in this life
and supremely happy with him forever.

If you are searching for a deeper peace in and around your
life, can I invite you to join me in an experiment with this
prayer? Please do not use it as a mindless mantra, or as some
kind of spiritual technique to get God to give you what you
want. I suggest that you use it in the following way:

First of all, make the prayer part of your daily devotions.
If you don't presently have a devotional time, begin by
setting aside a few minutes at the beginning of each day.
Pray the words of the Serenity Prayer from your heart.
Speak directly to God. Say the words with as much
thoughtfulness and attentiveness as possible. Think of
what you are facing in the coming day, as you pray.
Some people also find it helpful to use this prayer
together with the Lord's Prayer.

Secondly, write out the prayer on a small card and
try to memorise it. Carry the card around with you
during the day. Then, as you stand in a queue, or go
about your daily tasks, or go for a walk, or sit in a cof-

fee shop, you can let one or two of the phrases from the prayer go through your mind. You will be surprised, I believe, by the way God begins to work in your life.

Thirdly, you may like to find a prayer partner to share this prayer experiment with you. Or even a small group. Each week you could then come together and share the discoveries you are making as you learn to pray the Serenity Prayer on a regular basis. It may also be helpful, in these meetings together, to share some of your responses to the discussion starter at the end of each chapter. The spiritual journey is seldom private. We need each other.

I close this introduction with a simple thought. If we are going to be peacemakers in a strife-filled and unhappy world, we first have to seek peace within our own hearts and lives. We cannot share what we do not possess. May these meditations, therefore, guide you in your own quest for a deeper peace and serenity.

THE STORY BEHIND THE SERENITY PRAYER

Many people, when they heard that I was writing about the Serenity Prayer, asked me questions like: Where does it come from? Who wrote it? When did members of Alcoholics Anonymous begin to use it? How did it become so well known? At first I didn't know how to respond to these queries. So I began to do some research on the origins and use of the Serenity Prayer, and this is what I have found.

With regard to its authorship, no one can tell for sure who wrote it! Some theories trace it back to Boethius, a philosopher who lived around 500 AD, some think it was the work of an anonymous English poet, still others believe it was written by an American naval officer. What we do know is that its opening lines were used by Reinhold Niebuhr (1892–1971), a Protestant theologian who lectured for several years at the Union Theological Seminary in North America, at the beginning of a chapel address he gave in 1934. He used the following words which he credited to an 18th century theologian, Friedrich Oetinger:

God, give us the grace to accept with serenity
the things that cannot be changed,
courage to change the things which should be
    changed
And the wisdom to distinguish the one from the
    others.

In spite of following up a number of leads I have not been able to find out how the prayer developed from this formulation into its present more simple wording. Nor have I been able to discover how or when the remaining lines came to be added. I do know that in 1934 Dr Niebuhr's friend and neighbour, Dr Howard Robbins, asked permission to use these words in a compilation he was making at the time. It was published in that year in Dr Robbins' book of prayers.

In 1941 the opening lines of the prayer came to the attention of some AA members in New York. One of them came across a news clipping in the obituary column of the local newspaper, which read:

> Mother – God, grant me the serenity
> to accept the things I cannot change
> the courage to change the things I can
> and the wisdom to know the difference – goodbye.

These AA members felt that its emphases were particularly helpful in dealing not only with their own particular problems, but also with the great variety of life's difficulties and challenges. For several years the prayer was printed on small cards and dropped into every piece of mail that left the AA's office in Vesey Street, New York, and today it is often used in AA meetings. However, its main use seems to be that of a personal guide to prayer. Little wonder that the word "serenity" has become such an important word in the AA movement.

The rest, as they say, is history. Over the past 60 years the use of the prayer has gone far beyond AA boundaries. It has been translated into tens of different languages and is prayed by people from all kinds of backgrounds the world over. Today it is a prayer prayed literally by millions who find it to be a source of spiritual wisdom and guidance in their daily lives.

CHAPTER 1

GOD GRANT ME THE SERENITY

*T*HERE IS A SIMPLE PHRASE that often pops up in conversations. Its striking regularity intrigues me. Just last week, I heard it again. I was sitting with a thirty-something, a management consultant, celebrating his recent promotion. After sharing his good fortune and telling about his sense of elation and satisfaction, he suddenly sighed deeply. Then, with a wry smile, he said rather wistfully, "But there is still something missing in my life."

Whenever I hear those words, they remind me of that God-shaped vacuum inside all of us. A great void that only God can fill. Nothing else can. When we try to fill this empty space in our hearts with something other than God, our lives remain hollow. More than this, we experience an inner discontent that robs us of peace and serenity. Even though our lives may appear to be working well on the outside, on the inside we feel that there is something missing.

Perhaps you can identify with what I am trying to describe. Most of us, at some stage of our lives, sense this hollowness inside. Deep down we know that there is something missing, but we are not sure what to do about it. So we try different solutions. Perhaps we start going to gym, or attend a New Age course, or have an affair, or go out and buy something, or change our job, or take up a new hobby, or have a few more drinks. Some of these things help a little. Some more than others. But none of them seems to fill that aching void inside. And we are not at peace.

May I invite you to consider something? I want to suggest that this emptiness within our lives is one of God's most special gifts. A gift which reminds us that we all, whether religious or not, have an inborn desire for God. This desire is at the heart of our deepest longings. It can only be satisfied when we seek after God and have a personal relationship with God. Only then do we begin to experience true peace and serenity of heart and mind. Augustine, that great African saint, once said, many centuries ago, "God, you have made us for yourself and restless is our heart until it finds its rest in you."

WHAT IS SERENITY LIKE?

The first sentence of the Serenity Prayer connects with this deep longing. It invites us to turn towards God, as we are, and ask for the gift of serenity. Serenity is such a special word. It is a rich word that means far more than being happy, or having peace of mind, or knowing inner contentment, or not experiencing conflict. While it certainly carries some of these meanings, serenity is much more. To catch a glimpse of the richness and depth of this word it may be helpful to turn to something that Jesus once said to his followers. Just before he was put to death, he told them, "Peace I leave with you; my peace I give you. I do not give to you as the world gives."[1] Let us briefly look at these words.

On the one hand, there is the peace that the world gives. This refers to that fleeting kind of good feeling which comes when everything is going well. It is a pleasurable sense of well-being. I felt it the other day on holiday. Our family were at a holiday flat in Durban. We were sitting around a braai. The sun was setting, we could hear the sounds of the waves crashing onto the shore, and the smells of braaied meat hinted at the promise of a good meal. I felt tranquil, calm and content. This is the peace that the world gives. There is nothing wrong with it, but we all know that it can pass very quickly.

On the other hand, there is the peace that God gives. This is a spiritual peace, a peace that lasts and which cannot be taken away from us. It does not depend on everything going well. It is an inner assurance that, ultimately, all is well. Whether we are happy or not. Whether we get what we want or not. Whether we are satisfied with our circumstances or not. Whether we are burdened or not. It is a peace that goes beyond all human understanding. It cannot be grasped by the intellect alone. It is something that must be experienced in our hearts.

Perhaps the best picture of this peace can be seen in the life of Jesus himself. For most of his life, the odds were stacked against him. Few people really understood what he was about. His opponents were constantly out to get him. Even his friends let him down when he needed them the most. Tested, tried, taunted, Jesus managed to maintain an inner serenity through it all. He did not get mad at those who resisted him or who let him down. He did not give in to despair. He knew deep down that there was a good, loving, competent God whom he could trust completely. In the end all would be well.

RECEIVING THE GIFT OF SERENITY

Serenity, or peace as we have called it, comes as a gift from God. We cannot manufacture it. We will not find it outside of a real, genuine and growing relationship with God. The message of the Bible is unmistakingly clear. It goes like this. There is a God. This God is totally good, totally loving, totally competent. He has come to us in Jesus Christ whom we can totally trust. When we turn to this God with open hands, and ask for serenity, the gift of peace is given to us.

This does not mean that our lives are instantly filled with a deep, inner peace. Nor does it mean that there is nothing that we need to do from here onwards. When we pray the Serenity Prayer, the gift of peace comes as a seed, planted in our hearts. It still needs to be nurtured. At the very least, this will require us to face the different sources of unpeace in and around our lives, changing the way we think and live, and working for peace in the practical realities of our daily living. There is no lasting peace without effort. But when we do what we need to do, like a seed hidden in the soil, the gift of peace begins to germinate silently, and then bursts into flower in our lives and finally begins to bear fruit.

I end with a delightful story that illustrates the need for action. It is the story of a man who had a dream. Read the story as he tells it.

One night I had a dream. I walked to the marketplace and saw a stall with a sign, "Gifts of God". I stopped and saw an angel at the counter. Astonished, I asked, "What are you selling, dear angel?"

"Every gift that God gives."

"Are they expensive?"

"No, the gifts of God are free."

I looked at the shelves that were filled with jars of joy, bottles of patience, packets of wisdom. Finally, I saw the gift I wanted. I asked, "Please give me the gift of serenity."[2]

The angel kindly prepared everything in a small gift box. It was very tiny. Smaller than my heart. I asked, "Are you sure the gift is in there?"

"Yes, in God's shop we do not sell ripe fruit. Only seeds that you need to grow."

As we shall see in the following chapters, the rest of the Serenity Prayer shows us how we can grow the seed of serenity.

IN A NUTSHELL

Our hearts are filled with a restless longing that nothing on earth can ever fully satisfy. Only God can give us that deep, inner peace for which we yearn. In order to receive this gift, we need to enter into a trusting relationship with our Creator. When we take this step, the gift of peace is planted like a seed within us. It is our responsibility to ensure that this seed grows and bears fruit. How we go about doing this is what the Serenity Prayer is all about.

*What do you sense is missing from
your life at the moment?*

Peace I leave with you; my peace I give you. I do not give to you as the world gives. Do not let your hearts be troubled and do not be afraid.

JOHN 14:27

CHAPTER 2

TO ACCEPT THE THINGS
I CANNOT CHANGE

*H*AVE YOU EVER BEEN CAUGHT in a traffic jam? I guess we all have. A traffic jam is something we cannot change. We are powerless over it. I know a few people who travel in tortoise-like traffic each day, and who make the most of it. They listen to classical music, catch up on the news, play tapes, study, think positive thoughts, pray for those around them, and sometimes even sing. I call them saints! The majority of us get uptight, seethe, swear, pound the steering wheel or blow the hooter. None of these things helps. Our frustration simply builds up. We get angrier and more impatient as the time goes by.

Just the other day this happened to me. I was stuck on a nearby highway for almost two hours. Over the radio I heard that there had been an armed heist a few kilometres from where I was stationary, and that it would take a few hours to clear the road. Coming to a place of inner acceptance of what was happening was not easy. But when I did,

I felt a huge difference inside. I became less stressed, less frustrated and more relaxed. I was no longer trying to force unchangeable circumstances into a particular mould. Looking back, I can now see that I was experiencing something of the serenity that comes when we accept what cannot be changed.

Life can often be like this. Almost each day we find ourselves dealing with things that cannot be changed. Like traffic jams. The first suggestion that the Serenity Prayer makes is "to accept the things I cannot change". This kind of acceptance seldom comes easily. We need all the grace and help and power that God can give. But when we are able to accept what cannot be changed, the seed of peace planted in our hearts begins to germinate and grow. As time goes by, we gain the precious gift of serenity. With this in mind, let us explore three areas from our daily lives where this principle applies.

PAST REGRETS

Most of us carry regrets. There are many different kinds. Regrets of wasted opportunities and lost time. Regrets of things done and left undone. Regrets of decisions taken and those not taken. Regrets of words spoken and unspoken. Regrets like these rob us of our peace and serenity. Often they leave us with deep feelings of guilt or remorse, or even despair. We wish we could turn the clock back. But we cannot. Perhaps you will know, as I do, some of these painful effects that come from living with past regrets.

So what can we do? We can pray the Serenity Prayer. We can ask God to help us to accept the irreparable past. But we need to back up this prayer with a few things that we can do. Finding peace does not mean doing nothing. It may grow out of prayer, but it does not stop there. It brings new intentions, new obligations, new efforts. Let me share very briefly what I am learning to do with regard to some of my own past regrets. Especially those which have involved the hurting of those around me.

- I have found a few friends with whom I can be honest about these past regrets. These are friends who accept me "warts and all" and who do not try to fix me up.
- I am learning how to receive the forgiveness of God on a regular basis. Often I look at a cross, which represents God's forgiving love, and imagine God saying to me, "Trevor, see how much I love and forgive you."
- I am learning slowly how to make amends. Often an apology is all that is needed. Sometimes I need to do more. Sometimes I need to ask the person concerned what I need to do to make up for what I have done.

- If the regret concerns someone who has died, I often share with God my thoughts and feelings. I ask God to share them with the person concerned.

When it comes to making peace with past regrets, these are a few of the discoveries that I am making. You may like to add to the list those things that you have found helpful. When the Serenity Prayer is accompanied by actions like these, we open our hearts to the miracle of acceptance happening in our lives.

UNCHANGEABLE SITUATIONS

Earlier I referred to the traffic jam as an example of a circumstance that we cannot change. In comparison to some other unmanageable situations that we experience, a traffic jam is quite trivial. Others, however, can be deeply painful. Especially those that involve irreversible losses. The breakup of a close friendship. A divorce we don't want. The consequences of a severe stroke. The diagnosis of a terminal illness. The loss of a loved one through death. Traumatic losses like these cannot be reversed. And when they happen, they can make any talk about serenity sound almost perverse.

Yet, it is in these kinds of painful situations that the Serenity Prayer can become a close friend. Praying it in times of loss does not mean we must deny our grief. Or pretend to be tranquil. Losses need to be mourned. We need to befriend our tears, share our pain, express our anger. Grieving like this often leads us along that healing path towards a deeper peace. As we grieve we can still pray the Serenity Prayer and try to walk each day in its wisdom. We will find God slowly becomes more and more real to us. We sense that we are not alone. Acceptance gradually begins, bringing with it that precious gift of serenity. A grieving mother, who has been praying this prayer for a few months now, said to me the other day, "I'm slowly beginning to smile again through my tears."

OTHER PEOPLE

One of the hardest tendencies to overcome is our wanting to control and change other people. Often we want to straighten out those around us, fix them up and tell them what to do. If they happen to be feeling down and sad, we then want to make them happy. Those of us who profess to be following Jesus usually do this under the guise of wanting to be helpful and caring. Then, when those whom we are trying to change don't co-operate, we get uptight. If we are fortunate, the light begins to dawn for us that we really cannot change other people.

This does not mean that we cannot show others our care. But there is a huge difference between caring for others and trying to change them. Jane, a middle-aged woman in our congregation, made me aware of this again just the other day. For years she has been trying to get her husband to come to church. She has bargained with him, begged him, threatened him. All to no avail. About 18 months ago we had a conversation. We spoke together about the Serenity Prayer. She began to pray and live in its spiritual truths. She accepted the fact that she could not change or control her husband. She asked God to help her find ways to express the love she felt for him. Each day she placed her husband's life in God's hands. A little while ago we talked again. Listen to some of what she had to say.

"I really cannot believe the difference between now and the first time we talked. There is so much less tension and conflict in our relationship. We are enjoying each other so much more. And guess what, you won't believe this, but while you were away on holiday my husband came with me to church on Christmas Day. Without me asking him to do so. He said he enjoyed the service and may even come again."

Not all stories have such happy endings. There are times when a loved one's behaviour becomes dangerously self-destructive and abusive. Let us say that your spouse drinks far too much, regularly comes home drunk, and is often horrible in the way he or she speaks. The wisdom of the Serenity Prayer still applies. We cannot change the person. We can tell them that their behaviour is not acceptable. We can refuse to protect them from the consequences of their actions. We can join a Al-Anon group to find support. As we do all these things, their behaviour may continue. It may then become clear to us that the best thing we can do is to ask the person to leave, or we can separate until they have faced their problem, or we may need to end the relationship. Often we need to talk about these kinds of decisions with a wise companion.

IN A NUTSHELL

Accepting what cannot be changed, be it past regrets, unchangeable circumstances, or other people, leads us to serenity. As we have noticed, it can sometimes be very difficult to do this. That is why we pray the Serenity Prayer. We look beyond the strength of our willpower. We look towards the power that God alone can give us. While there may certainly be some things that we need to do, ultimately peace is a gift that God alone can give us. Especially the serenity to accept those things we cannot change.

What situation that cannot be changed do you find yourself struggling to accept?

TO ACCEPT THE THINGS I CANNOT CHANGE

But one thing I do: Forgetting

what is behind and straining

towards what is ahead, I press on

towards the goal to win the prize

for which God has called me

heavenwards in Christ Jesus.

PHILIPPIANS 3:13–14

CHAPTER 3

COURAGE TO CHANGE THE
THINGS I CAN

*A*FEW DAYS AGO I WAS CONFRONTED as I so often am
with my need to change. It happened during a conversation with Debbie. To put it politely, we were having a
domestic disagreement. It had been prompted by one of
those incidents that I sometimes think only happens in the
Hudson household. Let me explain.

One of our dogs had eaten some raw T-bone steaks
which were thawing in the sun. I was to braai them later for
our special Sunday lunch. Debbie, as you can well expect,
was upset. And she told me so. Rather than listening to
what she was feeling, I climbed in and accused her of allow-
ing her angry mood to affect us all. She became quiet. She
asked me whether my angry moods ever affected the family. "No they don't," I responded, "give me one example."

After saying this, I walked outside into the garden. I
stood by the burning charcoals and mulled over what had
just taken place. Out of the blue, some thoughts came into

33

my mind. They were clear, concise and challenging. They went like this. "Trevor you do have angry moods. They do affect those around you. Your response to Debbie was defensive, arrogant and self-righteous." I don't know whether they came from God or not. It certainly felt like they did. I went back inside, joined Debbie in the kitchen and apologised.

This experience underlines the importance of the second suggestion made by the Serenity Prayer. To ask for the courage to change the things we can. I needed to confront the challenge of dealing with my defensiveness, arrogance and self-righteousness. I am not the only one. All of us have these "character defects", as those in "twelve-step programmes" like to say. These things spoil our lives and our relationships. They need to be transformed. When they are, we also water and nourish the seed of peace. In our relationships at home, at our work places and in our communities. The burning question always is: How do we facilitate those inner changes which we so desperately need? (In a later chapter I will be dealing with changing those situations around us that need to be changed.)

ADMIT WHAT NEEDS TO CHANGE

Inner change begins when we actually face what it is that needs to change. Almost always it will be something that robs us of our serenity. Something that has become a source of discontent and conflict in our relationships. Something that adds to the tension in and around us. A number of things come to mind. It could be our always wanting to be in control, or our explosive temper, or our making rules for others that we don't keep ourselves, or our long-held resentments, or our not speaking the truth, or our deep-seated prejudices, or our wanting everything perfect around us, or, as it was in my case, needing to be in the right. When we are able to identify what needs to change, we are on the road to recovery.

It is not easy to come to this place of acknowledgement. More often than not we tend to deny what needs changing. Instead we criticise those around us. Blaming others then becomes the way we continue to avoid acknowledging what needs to be changed in ourselves. This is what was happening in my conversation with Debbie. Until those thoughts broke through my defences. These denial mechanisms are very much part of our lives. As a preacher once said, "Denial is not the name of a river in Egypt."

Until we overcome our deep-seated tendency to deny things, and begin to own the less attractive parts of our lives, we will not experience inner change. Progress along the spiritual pathway always requires that we grow in our knowledge of ourselves. This journey towards a greater self-honesty starts when we take a few simple steps.

- We can take some time to be quiet on a regular basis, just be ourselves, and ask God to search our hearts.
- We can reflect on our instant reactions to others, especially those that harm and do damage.
- We can look for in ourselves what we criticise in others.
- We can try to recognise those contradictions between what we are like at home, and what we are like in public.
- We can ask some friends who know us well to give us some feedback about how they find us. It is so easy to deceive ourselves. Our subjectivity can hide our most obvious character defects from our own eyes.

A word of encouragement. I have found that getting honest with myself and acknowledging what needs to change does not make me unacceptable to God. Nor does it make me feel far from God. Rather it opens my life, like few other things do, to the incredible depths of God's love and acceptance and mercy. I hope so much that this will be your experience as well.

LET GOD DO THE CHANGING

Over the years I have learned that inner change is not a do-it-yourself job. We all know what usually happens when we make resolutions, grit our teeth and try to change ourselves through our own willpower. We fail. While there may be a few outward changes for a short while, it is not long before the true condition of our hearts reveals itself. In fact, I have come to see that depending on our own strength seems to block real spiritual growth and change. We need a power that comes from beyond ourselves. As one slogan from Alcoholics Anonymous puts it, "We can't, God can, let him."

The wonderful news is that there is a good, loving and competent God who longs to help us become different. We don't have to go it on our own. That is why we pray the Serenity Prayer. The reason we need God, and a power from beyond ourselves, is that real change always flows from within. It is a matter of the heart. Inner change takes place in that hidden area of our lives which only God can reach and which we cannot see without God's help. It is God's Spirit alone who can bring about the change of heart that is our deepest need. When we truly realise this, it is like a heavy load being lifted from our back.

Let me say quickly that this does not mean we do nothing. When it comes to getting rid of our character defects, there is a need for careful effort on our part. As long as we don't try and do God's work. What we can do, as we have already seen, is to try to see and admit what needs to change. We can also express to God our desire for these character defects to be removed. One way we do this is by praying the Serenity Prayer regularly. When we pray these words, and really mean them, we are asking God to be our "heart transformer". Unless we do our part in these ways, it is unlikely that we will grow. But when we do face the truth of our lives, and allow the Spirit of God to change us, we slowly grow into the person God wants us to be.

Perhaps a picture will help to see this division of labour between God and ourselves more clearly. Imagine an escalator[1] going up to God. Whenever we find ourselves struggling with a particular character defect, for instance, always wanting to be in the right, we imagine ourselves picking it up as if it were a poisonous snake. We place it into a sack and put it on the escalator. When the sack comes back again, as it surely will, we have a quick look inside, see what it is, and place it back immediately. We get on with doing whatever we need to. We don't try to beat the character defect in our own strength. If we do, it will win each time. But every time it returns, we simply put it back on the escalator. After days, weeks, months or even years, we notice one day that it doesn't come back. We realise that God is in the process of changing us.

IN A NUTSHELL

A deep inner peace enters our lives when we acknowledge our need, turn to God and allow God to change us. As we have repeatedly noticed, this is not easy. It is difficult to face ourselves. To admit our faults. To recognise and accept our addictions. To put our pride in our pockets. To be ready to let God change us. That is why the Serenity Prayer invites us to pray for courage. The courage to set out on that never-ending journey of personal change and transformation. And when we do, we begin to experience that peace of heart and mind for which we are always looking.

*Name one character defect which you would
like to see changed in your life.*

COURAGE TO CHANGE THE THINGS I CAN

Why do you look at the speck

of sawdust in your brother's

eye and pay no attention to

the plank in your own eye?

How can you say to your

brother, "Let me take the

speck out of your eye," when

all the time there is a plank in

your own eye?

MATTHEW 7:3-4

CHAPTER 4

WISDOM TO KNOW THE DIFFERENCE

WHEN WE BEGIN TO PRAY THE Serenity Prayer, it will not be long before we begin to experience some difficult dilemmas. Usually they come in those kinds of situations where we are torn between two choices. Either to accept whatever it is that we are facing, or to try to change it. Having to decide in matters like these can often rob us of serenity and peace. We find ourselves sleeping badly, or unable to concentrate, or constantly experiencing a knot in our stomachs. Recently I have been talking with a number of people struggling in this regard. Here are some examples:

A woman married for 24 years speaks about her complete lack of sexual desire for her husband. She tells me that there has been no spark between the two of them for several years. She feels her marriage has become a sham. The children have now left home and she dreads the possibility of a loveless future. She has tried professional therapy, medication, and healing prayer, all to little avail. She wonders whether she should accept the situation for what it is, try again to change her feelings or consider the route of divorce.

A mother and father share a deep concern for their 17-year-old son. Recently he has been making choices that represent values very different from their own. It has caused great tension in the home. Now they are asking, must they accept their son for who he is, along with his different values, or try to influence him by talking about their own strongly held values more forcibly? Do they seek to be an example only, or do they try to legislate their son's morality?

A lawyer in his early 40s talks about his vocational crisis. The law firm where he works has priorities that clash with some of his own hopes for the future. He is uncertain about what route to take. Should he accept the prevailing work culture and try to adapt? Does he need to try to change it, even if it causes tension? Or is it time to take a risk, make a complete break and set up his own business?

Scenarios like these are common. Perhaps you are able to think of a similar situation from your own life. One where you struggle with whether to accept or whether to change something. As we can see in the above examples, it is not always easy to find the best way forward. We need wisdom. This is precisely what the Serenity Prayer invites us to pray for.

THE WISDOM WE NEED

The wisdom we need goes deeper than knowledge. While it is unlikely that we can be wise without some learning, knowledge by itself is not wisdom. We can see this very easily. There are people who possess outstanding academic qualifications, hold down highly-paid jobs, and have prominent profiles, but who would struggle to pass "Grade One" when it comes to relationships and living a happy and genuinely peaceful life. Let's face it. Knowledge alone is not enough to meet life's challenges and problems. We need something more. We need wisdom.

Wisdom, in contrast to knowledge alone, is knowing how to use wisely what we know. It is being able to sift through different options, distinguish true from false, discriminate between good and evil and choose the best way forward. It is when we walk down this path of wisdom, that we start to make the most of our short lives here on earth. We deal with conflict more effectively. We have more satisfying relationships. We make better choices. We live more at peace with ourselves, others and with God. In a nutshell, we discover life at its fullest.

I am sure you are asking, "How do we get this wisdom?" After all, we all know how to get information: we read books; we enrol for study courses; we surf the net; we watch talk shows; we listen to tapes; we consult experts. But how do we go about becoming wiser? Especially when trying to decide whether to accept something or to try to change it.

Over the years, with the help of some trusted spiritual mentors and teachers, a simple three-step process of discernment has become clearer for me. It has helped me enormously in moments of decision-making. I hope you will also find it helpful.

ASK GOD

The Serenity Prayer reminds us that true wisdom is a gift that comes from God. It is something we need to pray for. Certainly the Scriptures tell us to do this. "If any of you is lacking in wisdom, ask God, who gives to all generously and ungrudgingly, and it will be given you."[1] The wisdom we so desperately need cannot be bought, or earned, or invented. It is given by God and must be asked for. "Dear God," we can simply pray, "I need your wisdom. Please speak to me, through my friends, through the Bible and whatever else I may read, through the experiences I have today, and through circumstances."

Asking God for wisdom in this way does not mean that we will automatically get our answer in bright neon lights. Or that everything will work out smoothly, neatly and tidily. Nor does it imply that wisdom will drop into our lives from heaven while we put our feet up. As we shall soon see, besides asking God for wisdom, there are also some things that we need to do. And when we support our prayer request for wisdom with these practical measures, we will find that God does begin to show us the way and bless us with wisdom.

The guidance we need usually comes gradually. My experience is that we receive just enough to know what to do next. Like a hand-held lamp that lights up the next few steps along a dark pathway, God gives us just enough light to keep us walking. As we step into the light that we have been given, another bit of illumination comes along, guiding us further. And so we proceed. Step by step. Sometimes accepting what cannot be changed, at other times seeking to change what we can. All the time trusting that God lovingly walks with us.

LISTEN TO OUR THOUGHTS
AND FEELINGS

Once we have asked God for wisdom to know whether to accept or to change something, we get on with our lives and do what needs to be done. Except that we now consciously place ourselves into a listening mode. By this I mean that we begin to pay attention to what goes on in our lives and minds and hearts. When we do this, we will find there is a clamour of different intuitions and desires, thoughts and feelings, longings and hopes within us. It is always a good habit to write these things down so that we can reflect on them a little more. Normally when God does speak to us, the divine voice takes the shape of one of these inner promptings. So unless we listen carefully to what is happening within our lives we can so easily miss the whisperings of the Spirit.

If nothing seems to stand out in our mind, we don't get alarmed. We simply repeat our need for wisdom, continue with what we have to do, and confidently get on with our lives. But we continue to listen in the way outlined above. We also constantly remind ourselves that God is totally good, totally loving, and totally competent. We don't need to try to force God's hand into giving us some direction or we will probably end up doing our will and not God's. We rest in the quiet assurance that if God has something to share with us, God will share it in a way that we can understand.

During this listening phase it might also be useful to discuss the whole situation with trusted friends. Other people's view of things can help us see the overall picture of our lives more clearly and give us perspective on the steps we need to take. This is one important reason why we need companions on the spiritual journey. God often speaks to us through the words of those around us. Sometimes they confirm what we are already thinking, or bring a view that we have not yet considered.

MAKE A DECISION

The old Quakers had a wonderful way of making decisions. They believed that God really wants to guide us when we are faced with difficult dilemmas. They taught that God does this in a simple way. After we have asked God for wisdom, we check first of all that the matter we are dealing with is not settled by the clear teaching of the Bible. If it is not, we then pay attention to whatever is going on inside us, as outlined above. Once we have done this, we take the following step:

Using our imagination we see ourselves making one possible decision. Let us say that it is the option of accepting whatever it is we are facing. We see ourselves with our mind's eye continuing to live in the situation just as it is, and not trying to change it. Then we hold this picture before us for a few moments before we let it fade. As it fades, we become aware of how we are feeling.

Next, we see ourselves deciding the other way. In this case, trying to change the situation in some way. We imagine ourselves doing our best to make some sort of difference. We hold the picture of ourselves doing this before us, before letting it fade away. Again, we monitor our inner responses to this possible scenario. Do we feel at peace? Or are we anxious, unsettled, uneasy?

The Quakers believed that a deeper peace would rest on the decision that God wanted us to make. Not excitement, or thrills, or an adrenalin rush, but a quiet steady peace or serenity. This inner assurance would be God's way of guiding us, even if it was the more difficult and painful path. People of faith have constantly reminded us throughout the centuries that God always leads us in peace. However, even if we do believe that God has guided us, we do not claim infallibility for our decision. Phrases like "God told me" are not helpful. It is far better to take personal responsibility for our decision and to leave open the possibility that we may be wrong.

IN A NUTSHELL

We receive the gift of serenity when we allow God's wisdom to guide our lives. Particularly when it comes to deciding whether we must change something. This wisdom comes when we ask God for it, reflect on our thoughts and feelings and make a decision. When we follow the choice on which a deep peace rests, we will find the way that God wants us to go.

Specify one area of your present life situation where you are needing God's wisdom.

If any of you lacks wisdom,

he should ask God, who gives

generously to all without

finding fault, and it will be

given to him.

JAMES 1:5

CHAPTER 5

LIVING ONE DAY AT A TIME

M ANY RECOVERING ALCOHOLICS make use of a small pamphlet entitled, "Just for today". At the back are written the first few sentences of the Serenity Prayer. On the inside are several guidelines about living one day at a time.

This little leaflet has been an inspiration to many who are struggling to overcome their alcohol addiction. But its relevance is not limited to alcoholics alone. It also has great meaning for all who want to live more peaceful, serene and sane lives. In case you have not come across it yet, it goes like this:

- Just for today… I will try to live through this day only, and not tackle my whole life problem at once. I can do something for twelve hours that would appal me if I had to keep it up for a lifetime.
- Just for today… I will be happy. This assumes to be true what Abraham Lincoln said, that, "Most folks are as happy as they make up their minds to be."

- Just for today... I will adjust myself to what is, and not try to adjust everything to my own desires. I will take my "luck" as it comes, and fit myself to it.
- Just for today... I will try to strengthen my mind. I will study. I will learn something useful. I will not be a mental loafer. I will read something that requires effort, thought and concentration.
- Just for today... I will exercise my soul in three ways: I will do somebody a good turn, and not get found out; if anybody knows of it, it will not count. I will do at least two things I don't want to do – just for exercise. I will not show anyone that my feelings are hurt: they may be hurt, but today I will not show it.
- Just for today... I will be agreeable. I will look as well as I can, dress becomingly, talk low, act courteously, criticise not one bit, not find fault with anything, and not try to improve or regulate anybody except myself.
- Just for today... I will have a programme. I may not follow it exactly but I will have it. I will save myself from two pests: hurry and indecision.
- Just for today... I will have a quiet half-hour all by myself, and relax. During this half-hour, some time, I will try to get a better perspective of my life.

- Just for today… I will be unafraid. Especially I will not be afraid to enjoy what is beautiful, and to believe that as I give to the world, so the world will give to me.

You might like to get a copy from your nearest group of Alcoholics Anonymous, or even write down these words for yourself and carry them around with you. You will discover, as I have, that they provide wonderful ideas about how we can put into practice the invitation of the Serenity Prayer to live one day at a time.

DAILY RESOLUTIONS

These suggestions underline the value of making daily resolutions. This thought may come as a surprise. We are much more accustomed to making annual resolutions than daily ones. While we obviously need to develop yearly plans for our lives, we can also learn to make each day "a New Year's Day". Each day then becomes a new beginning of new beginnings. We can decide specifically, "Today I will do this… Today I will do that." In this way we can make daily resolutions which will help us to live more freely and fully.

This is what most recovering alcoholics have learned to do. They generally don't make decisions "never" to drink again. Rather, they resolve to stay sober for the next 24 hours. One day at a time. You and I can also learn to live on this basis. One or two simple daily resolutions, like the ones described in the leaflet, can contribute enormously to our spiritual, emotional and physical well-being. They provide us with a practical, down-to-earth means of reaching out for that peace which our hearts so deeply desire.

I am sure I can hear you saying, isn't the road to hell paved with good intentions? It may be. We all know people who say that they intend doing certain things which they never do. Perhaps you and I are among them. Of course, sometimes there are outside circumstances beyond our control that work against our intentions. Or there may be internal feelings and habits that make it very difficult for us to implement our resolutions. It is for these very reasons that we back up our intentions by praying the Serenity Prayer. Knowing that we may struggle to live differently, we ask God for the strength and the power we need to put our daily resolutions into practice.

You can start right away. Read the "Just for today" suggestions again. Which one most connects with you? It might be that you are struggling with a particular problem. Perhaps you want to stop smoking. Or reduce your dependence on tranquillisers. Or stay away from the casino. Or overcome some other addiction. Then the first resolution concerning tackling our problems on a "one day at a time" basis may be the one for you. Or it could be that you are feeling depressed and sad right now. Then the last resolution about enjoying what is beautiful may need to be applied in your life.

Maybe none of these resolutions is relevant for you. Then why not make up one that does? Recently I have made a decision not to always have the last word. It has been wonderfully liberating.

NIGHTLY REVIEWS

Another habit that can help us to live one day at a time is the nightly review.[1] About twelve years ago I was introduced to a very simple way of doing this. Of all my personal spiritual practices this one has brought the most growth. I usually do it on my own just before I fall asleep, but it can also be done with a loved one, or even the whole family. The process has three simple steps, each one flowing into the next. It can last anything between a few minutes and half-an-hour.

- Make some time to be quiet for a few moments. Take a few deep breaths to settle down. Invite God to be with you and to shed light on the past day.
- Ask God to bring to mind one moment of the day for which you are most grateful. The moment which gave

you the most life. Or when you received or gave the most love. If you could recapture one moment, which would it be? Relive this moment. Breathe in again the gratitude you felt, and thank God for it.

• Ask God to bring to mind the moment you are least grateful for. The moment which drained you of life. Or when you received and gave the least love. Reflect on what was said and done at that moment which made it so hard. Acknowledge your feelings about this experience. Refrain from judging yourself. Share these feelings with God and let God's love fill you again.

Doing this review every night can bring immense benefits. It can help us to keep tabs on those character defects which we are wanting to see changed. It can encourage us in the future to do less of what harms us and others, and more of what gives life to us and to others. It can keep us in tune with the presence and guidance of God in the different aspects of our everyday lives. Generally speaking, we can be very sure that God wants us to give ourselves more to what gives us life, wherever possible, than to what drains us. Most importantly, the consistent practice of this nightly review can help us to embark more creatively on the adventure of living one day at a time.

IN A NUTSHELL

The Serenity Prayer invites us to ask God to help us live "just for today". This does not mean that we must stop setting goals. Or that we must quit planning for our future. Or that we must cancel our insurance policies. It simply expresses our desire to focus on this day, and allow it to absorb most of our energy, effort and interest. When we begin to live this way, we find ourselves building better foundations for the future, as well as knowing that our yesterdays have been well lived. We will also discover a far greater peace and serenity.

What keeps you from living one day at a time?

LIVING ONE DAY AT A TIME

Therefore do not worry about tomorrow, for

tomorrow will worry about itself. Each day

has enough trouble of its own.

MATTHEW 6:34

CHAPTER 6

ENJOYING ONE MOMENT
AT A TIME

*T*HERE IS A WONDERFUL STORY about a wise man who is being pursued by a bear. He literally runs off a cliff. As he is falling, he grabs a branch. He looks up and sees the bear leaning over the cliff, clawing at his head, just missing it each time. As he looks down to the ground below, only a few centimetres away, he sees a ferocious lion leaping up, missing his dangling feet. As he looks at the branch he is clutching, he sees two groundhogs gnawing away at it. He watches as his lifeline disappears, bite by bite.

As he takes a long, deep breath, he notices growing out of the cliff side, a clump of wild strawberries. In the midst of the clump there is a great, red, juicy strawberry. With his one free hand, he reaches over, picks the strawberry, puts it in his mouth, chews it slowly and says, "Ah, delicious, the best strawberry I've ever tasted in my whole life."

Whenever we ask God to help us to enjoy one moment at a time, as the Serenity Prayer suggests we do, it may be

59

helpful to remember this story. It invites us to savour the present moment, to immerse ourselves in it, and to live it to the fullest. It reminds us that, when we do live with a sense of immediacy, there are gifts to be discovered. One of these is God's gift of peace. Enjoyment of the present moment and the genuinely peaceful heart go together, hand in glove.

THE IMPORTANCE OF THE
HERE AND NOW

If we are going to enjoy the present moment, we first need to be convinced about its importance. Too often we allow ourselves to be preoccupied with the past or the future. We struggle to live wholeheartedly in the present. Like a ping-pong ball that goes from one side of the table to the other, our minds constantly bounce between yesterday and tomorrow. We need to catch this ball, hold it lightly and give this moment our full attention. Strengthening our belief that what is most important is the here and now will encourage us to attempt this. Here are two thoughts that may deepen this conviction for you.

First of all, the here and now is all that we have. We can visit the past, imagine the future, but we cannot live in either of these two places. Our lives happen minute by minute, second by second, moment by moment. It is in the here and now that our lives and Life intersect. For this reason the present moment is something very precious. We will never get another chance to live in it. It is unrepeatable. A deeply sacred gift from God.

Someone has said that the words "nowhere" and "now here" have the same arrangement of letters. The difference between these words is a small space. Likewise, we can either experience our lives as nowhere or now here. When we are preoccupied with the past or the future, we disconnect ourselves from the present moment. No longer do we live in the here and now. As the Beatles once sang, we become nowhere people living in a nowhere land.

Secondly, the here and now becomes even more important when we realise that it is the place where God meets us. We encounter God in the present, or we don't encounter God at all. If we are going to experience the peace that God gives, this gift needs to be received in the immediacy of the present moment. Whatever it may be like. Glad or sad. High or low. Difficult or easy. It is only in the here and now that we are in the presence of God. Now is always the acceptable time for us to receive the gifts that God wants to give.

This could be why Jesus said that, if we are going to experience God, we need to become like little children.[1] Children live totally in the present. Next time you walk past a playground, take some time to look at the kids. Watch them playing with each other. Notice how simple things like throwing and catching a ball, playing hide and seek, riding on the swings, capture all their attention. Observe the absence of hurry. Once upon a time, you and I were like that. Able to enjoy the present moment. The good news is that we can rediscover this gift.

LEARNING TO ENJOY THE
PRESENT MOMENT

It is not easy to live fully in the here and now. I realised this again recently. During a supper discussion, my daughter suddenly interrupted my thoughts, when she repeated, "Earth calling Dad. Earth calling Dad. Come in Dad." She had sensed that, although I was physically present, my mind was somewhere else. Her honest expression of frustration jolted me back to the present moment. She had made me aware again of how easily I disengage myself from enjoying and involving myself in what is before me.

We need to relearn how to enjoy and delight in the present moment. No one else can do this for us. The present moment is a special gift that we are either there to receive, or we are not. If we miss it, it is gone forever.

Fortunately, there are those around us more practised in the art of living in the here and now. Often they are people who have suffered a great deal. If we are wise, we will listen to them. Let me introduce you to three such people who have touched my life, and share what they have taught me.

SLOW DOWN

Some years ago a dear friend suffered a heart attack. It has changed his life radically. One of the things he has had to face was to banish hurry from his life. It has not been easy. Long-held habits of workaholism, haste and impatience are difficult to get rid of. Each day he recommits himself to a slower pace of life. He has learned to rest more regularly, eat less hurriedly, plan his day more carefully and rush less. He prays and meditates on the Serenity Prayer as often as he can. In a recent testimony he testified to what this practice of slowing down had meant to him. He said simply, "I have found a new peace by learning to enjoy each moment as it comes."

There is a saying, "Hurry is not of the devil; it is the devil." Maybe you think this is an exaggerated claim. Well, if it is the devil's intention to spoil our lives, as the Bible tells

us it is, then hurry could well be one of his best nicknames.[2]
Consider, as a brief example, the effects of hurry on our
lives. It makes it very difficult for us to be really aware of
what is happening in and around us. It diminishes our
capacity to give our full attention to those that we are with.
It limits our ability to invest ourselves totally in whatever
task we are doing. In a nutshell, it makes present-focused
living almost impossible. The first step towards overcoming
these effects, and recovering our enjoyment of each
moment, is the practice of slowing down.

SAY THANK YOU MORE OFTEN

A young woman who died of leukaemia when she was 25
taught me this. For almost three years she struggled with the
disease. During this time we often shared together, read
Scripture together, prayed together. On a cold winter's
evening, I visited her at home. She greeted me warmly at
the door, a gown wrapped around her frail body, and invited
me inside. She made coffee, toasted some hot-cross buns,
buttered them and brought them to where I was sitting at
the kitchen table. As she did this, I will never forget her
words, "You know, when you have been through what I
have been through, you say thank you for everything, even
coffee and hot-cross buns."

When we were small children, we had this capacity to say thank you for the good things in our lives. Have you ever listened to a child say grace? They go on for ever. "Thank God for the food, and the dog, and the cat, and the butterflies, and the sky and the grass, and my teddy…" One day, without realising it, the gratitude suddenly goes away. It's just, "Give me the jam". If we are fortunate, we can rediscover this capacity for saying thank you before we die. We become like little children again, appreciating the goodness of God in every good thing we experience. We fill the present moment with spontaneous expressions of gratitude and thankfulness. Even when, like for my dear friend, it does not quite rate a ten.

REALISE OUR MORTALITY

The other day a woman came to see me. Her husband has recently been diagnosed with cancer. The prognosis was that he had two to five years to live. I asked how this news had affected their relationship. Her response took me by surprise. She shared at length about the deeper intimacy they were experiencing. How they had grown closer in this past month than in all their previous 28 years together. One thing she said stood out for me. "We make sure that we enjoy every moment that we have together. We share more, laugh more, cry more. Even though it has brought lots of sadness, the prognosis has been a gift to our relationship."

When we realise how short life is, it can become a wonderful gift. Far from making us morbid, it will encourage us to make some immediate changes to the way we live and relate. Changes that will enable a richer delight and enjoyment in the present moment. Changes like spending more time with the special people in our lives. Or forgiving someone that we have hurt. Or resurrecting a buried talent like piano playing or painting. Or giving away some of our material resources. Or beginning a real relationship with God. These are the kinds of life-giving changes that take place when we realise that we are not going to be on earth for ever. Little wonder the Bible encourages us to see our physical lives "as a mist that appears for a little while, and then vanishes."

IN A NUTSHELL

Most of us live too much in the fast lane. When Friday evening comes around we wonder where the week has gone. Everything seems a blur. Against this backdrop of our busy lives, the Serenity Prayer steers us towards the importance of the here and now. It is in the present moment that God wants to give us the gift of peace. To receive it we need to slow down, live gratefully, and accept that we have only one life to live. Maybe then, even with the bear above us, a lion beneath and the groundhogs chewing away at our life-lines, we will enjoy the strawberry.

How can you learn to enjoy the present moment?

ENJOYING ONE MOMENT AT A TIME

Be very careful, then, how you live – not as

unwise but as wise, making the most of every

opportunity, because the days are evil.

EPHESIANS 5:15–16

CHAPTER 7

ACCEPTING HARDSHIPS AS THE PATHWAY TO PEACE

O NE OF THE BEST-SELLING BOOKS of the last two decades has been Scott Peck's *The Road Less Travelled*. Literally millions of people from all around the world have learned wonderful lessons from it. Without wanting to distract from its thoughtful content, I have a strong suspicion that one of the reasons for the book's widespread popularity is its opening line. It begins with the simple yet profound assertion, "Life is difficult."

This sentence strikes a deep responsive chord in our hearts. Life can be hard. None of us escapes pain or grief or loneliness. We know this from experience. Think for a moment of some of the hardships that come our way: loved ones get sick, our marriages go through rough patches, children go off the rails, finances get tight, business ventures fail, retrenchments take place, friends let us down, and the list goes on. When difficulties like these come along, life can become very tough.

Even when life seems to be going well on the outside, we can experience deeper troubles. Indeed, it is often when the external difficulties of life are removed that we have to face the deepest struggles of our souls. It could be a struggle with depression, or the stifling pain of shame, or the longings of an empty heart, or the anguish of an immense grief and loss. These hidden difficulties are as real as the outward ones, and sometimes even tougher.

Right now you may be going through some of these struggles. If not, you can be sure that there will come a time when you will. Sooner or later, troubles come to all of us. What matters most is how we decide to respond to them. We have two choices before us. On the one hand we can try to avoid them. On the other hand, as the Serenity Prayer suggests, we can ask God to help us to accept them as the pathway to peace. Let us explore these two alternatives more deeply.

AVOIDANCE BEHAVIOURS

If we are honest we will realise that we have many different ways, often very subtle, of avoiding facing up to our problems. We all do these things to a greater or lesser degree. As I have reflected on the ways in which I have personally tried to skirt around problems in my own life and the painful feelings associated with them, let me suggest a few of the possible avoidance techniques we sometimes use in these situations. See if you can identify the ways in which you sometimes do this. When we are able to identify our own particular method of evading our struggles, it can help us to find more creative ways of dealing with the hardships of our lives.

BLAMING

When we find ourselves in a difficult situation, it is very easy to blame others. "If it were not for my poor upbringing, I could have done better with my life." "If you hadn't distracted me the accident would not have happened." "If you were more loving our marriage could have been better." Blamers are usually people who don't like to take responsibility. They like to insist that the cause for their difficulties lies beyond themselves. While we are certainly not responsible for everything that happens, trying to distinguish that for which we are to blame is one of the deepest challenges that life puts in front of us.

IGNORING

Sometimes we try to avoid problems by ignoring them. Rather than accepting that they exist, like the proverbial ostrich we bury our heads in the sand. We hope that they will go away of their own accord. We refuse to confront them, reflect on what may be causing them, and solve them. But these things seldom just disappear. They have to be acknowledged, accepted and addressed. Otherwise they will forever remain a barrier to peace and serenity in our lives, relationships and communities.

ADDICTION

Often we try to "escape" by getting involved with addictive substances or behaviours. There are many ways of doing this. We might drink more than we should. Or dull our senses with the excessive use of tranquillisers. Or eat compulsively. Or immerse ourselves in long hours of work. Or fill our lives with religious activities. At first these things may temporarily lift our mood and help us feel a little better about ourselves. But then one day the problems caused by our addictive behaviour become more of a problem than the difficulties we are trying to avoid. If we are fortunate, this is when we wake up to the wisdom of the Serenity Prayer and accept our hardships as the pathway to peace.

SOME GOOD NEWS

Whenever we find ourselves experiencing difficulties, there is one bit of good news that we need to hold on to. Put very simply, it is this: God is deeply present in all the facts of our lives. Even when they are painful. There is no fear, no loss, no grief, no loneliness, no despair, no addiction, no desolation, no suffering which God does not share in. God is continually present and reaching out to us in whatever we may be going through at this moment.[1] When we know that God is with us, even when our world is falling apart, we are more able to face the pain of things with hope and courage.

I remember learning this again from the words of a courageous and grieving mother. It was during a weekend silent retreat for first-time retreatants. Late on the Saturday evening I spent some time listening to this mother whose 19-year-old son had been killed in a car accident. Her suffering was immeasurable and went far beyond the comfort of any human words. She had just spent time in a darkened chapel looking at a stark crucifix. She told me simply, "I can face tomorrow because I know that God shares my suffering and my pain."

Can you now see more clearly why the Serenity Prayer asks us not to run away from our hardships? They are the place where the Suffering God draws close to us. God can only bless us where we actually are, especially when we are going through tough times. If we constantly try to escape our pain, we can easily miss the gifts that God wants to bless us with. Gifts like peace and serenity and growth. But when we face these testing moments head on, with the confidence that Someone is there going through them with us, we open ourselves to receive whatever good thing God may bestow on us.

SMALL STEPS TOWARDS ACCEPTANCE

You may be wondering what this acceptance involves, especially in the light of the particular hardships life has thrown at you. Does it mean having to accept them with passive resignation, throwing up our hands, doing nothing, leaving everything to God? Or does it mean something very different? These are important questions. They deserve our best thinking and reflection. Here are some small steps that may lead us into a deeper acceptance of our hardships as the pathway to peace.

- We can take some time to look at the cross. This is where we see what God's love is really like. The mystery of the cross reminds us that God is no stranger to human pain. Not only does God understand our suffering, God shares it. We are never alone in our pain. It is this truth that keeps the light of faith flickering in our broken hearts; renews hope in our grieving; and rekindles loving in hearts that have been betrayed and broken.

- We can affirm that God is present with us in our painful and difficult situations. We can say to ourselves, "This situation is where God is wanting to meet and bless me." This simple affirmation can help us to see every difficult situation as an opportunity for God's goodness, love and competence to become a reality in our experience. It can also open our hearts to receive God's gifts of serenity and peace.

- We can find another person to be our "wailing wall". Someone who can listen to our stories of struggle without trying to change or fix us. Few things prove more helpful in times of great difficulty than to have another human being come alongside our lives and bear our pain with us. Such a friend becomes an open channel of God's love and care.

- We can choose to be gentle with ourselves. Often when we go through hard times, we can be very hard on ourselves. "If only I had done...this would not have happened." "I must have done something wrong to have brought this awful thing about." Refraining from these kinds of negative self-accusations can help us keep our sense of worth and dignity, even when things go badly wrong.

- We can ask God for the strength to do something constructive when we are tempted to give up. It could be something very simple, such as walking around the block, making ourselves a cup of tea, taking a walk in the garden or phoning a good friend. A purely passive diversion like reading or watching television is usually not enough to rouse us out of our darkness and depression. We need to act by summoning all our courage and doing something simple and creative.

IN A NUTSHELL

I have not found it easy to write this chapter because I am deeply aware that many reading these words face almost unbearable hardships. But I do know, from the witness of many courageous people around me, that we can experience God's presence in moments of deep pain. When we do, we are able to take small steps towards acceptance. Each of these steps is like a candle burning in the dark. It does not take the darkness away, but it guides us through, along the pathway of peace.

What difference would it make to you if you knew that God was deeply present in all the facts of your life?

Consider it pure joy, my brothers, whenever you

face trials of many kinds, because you know that

the testing of your faith develops perseverance.

JAMES 1:2–3

CHAPTER 8

TAKING, AS HE DID,
THE SINFUL WORLD AS IT IS,
NOT AS I WOULD HAVE IT

*I*HAVE RECENTLY BEEN COLLECTING some headlines from our daily newspapers. It has been a sobering experience. Many of them are grim reminders of the dark world we live in. Here are some that have stood out for me:

"Serial killer appears in court"
"Young woman abducted during hijacking"
"Hidden rape horrors behind prison bars"
"Intimidation at the polls"
"White collar crime figures soar"
"More civilians killed in Middle East conflict"

Headlines like these often have a negative impact on us. They contribute to increasing levels of anxiety and fear. They remind us of our deeply ingrained tendency toward wrong-doing. They tempt us to become cynical, bitter and hostile. And for those who are seeking to walk along that pathway to peace, they raise a burning question, "How can we live in a positive way in the midst of the evil and sin that surrounds us?"

This part of the Serenity Prayer meets us right at the centre of this question. It begins by acknowledging the reality of a sinful world. It also proposes adopting a particular attitude towards it. It is a stance which springs from the way God relates to our world. In order for us to imagine what it may mean to adopt a similar attitude, let us first explore God's approach and then tease out what it may mean for us to live in his Spirit.

GOD'S ATTITUDE TOWARDS
THE WORLD

It is striking that, even though the condition of the world must break God's heart, he does not condemn it. One of the most significant verses in this regard comes from John's Gospel. It says that God did not send his Son into the world to condemn it, but to save it.[1] In other words, God didn't go to all the trouble of sending his Son to point an accusing finger or to tell the world how bad it was. He came to help, to restore, to heal and to put the world right again. And

God did this, as the Serenity Prayer points out, by "taking the sinful world as it is".

This statement also underlines the way God accepts us, "warts and all". When we are being faithful and when we are not. Although God longs to see his dream realised in our lives, he does not use the method of condemnation as a way to bring it about. People always seem to react negatively to a spirit of condemnation. Only the way of positive acceptance changes human hearts. Therefore God continues to love us even when we say or think or do evil things. This point is brought home forcibly by the cross where, in spite of all the evil that was done to Jesus, nothing could stop him loving and accepting people.

This unconditional acceptance does not imply that God condones evil. We can see in the life of Jesus that he does not. Throughout his ministry Jesus sought to overcome evil with good. He started with himself, facing his own temptations and resisting them. He forgave people who were paralysed by sin. He freed those in the grip of demonic forces. He welcomed the marginalised. He cleansed the temple of crooked moneylenders. Through these actions, and similar others, he left no doubt about God's attitude when people were harmed or in need. God's heart goes out to them and he seeks to act for good on their behalf.

How do we reflect God's attitude in our everyday lives? A recent conversation with a concerned mother brought this question into sharp focus for me. She explained the situation she finds herself in right now. Her son has just opened what is called "a gentlemen's club". Nightly entertainment consists of strippers, lap dancers, topless waitresses and escort services. Her faith cannot condone what her son is doing. Yet she wants to stay connected to him. How can she do this, she asks, without appearing to be "holier than thou"?

For almost an hour we talked together. I told her about the Serenity Prayer and mentioned the sentence that is at the heart of this chapter. We looked at how God responds when his values conflict with ours. Together we wondered aloud what this could mean for her. Several guidelines emerged as we reflected on God's attitude. She seemed to find them helpful for the dilemma she was experiencing. You may find that they shed light on a problematic situation that you are facing at the moment. Let me share them with you.

DO NOT CONDEMN

If we want to reflect God's attitude, we need to give up being judgemental. Remember, Jesus said, "Judge not."[2] These words invite you and me to become the kind of person who lives beyond the condemnation of others. He wanted his followers to have the kind of hearts that would accept people as they are. He saw that condemnation rarely, if ever, brings about the change that it seeks. More often than not it conveys to the judged person the painful message, "You are not acceptable", or "I do not like you".

One reason for not judging, as Jesus pointed out, is that there is often a counter-attack if we do. We can be sure that if the mother expresses condemnation of her son's business venture, he will soon find something to attack in her. Most probably it will be some area where she is not quite living up to the values that she holds. We are all aware of how easily this happens. For example, if you are a parent, and you confront your teenage child for drinking, what happens? Before long you find yourself condemned for coffee, or tobacco, or tranquilliser use; or for something else that equals drinking in your child's eyes.

LOVE THE SINNER, HATE THE SIN

Many people struggle with this statement. How can I disapprove of what someone is doing, yet still love them? Especially if what they are doing is hurting me and others that I love. How can you separate a person from their actions?

Our example, of course, comes from God. As we have seen, God loves people without conditions, but does not approve of every kind of human behaviour. We can have no doubt that God stands utterly opposed to things like corruption, violence, injustice, sexual exploitation and all other expressions of evil. These things go totally against God's essential nature of goodness. They also undermine the love God intends us to have for one another.

But this does not mean that God ever rejects people or gives up on them. God will continue to love us and hold out his arms to us, even if we sin very seriously. And you and I can also do this in our relationships with others, although it may be very difficult. It is possible, with God's help, to draw a line between the person and their sinful actions. It is not easy and we will have to pray very hard. But it is possible. God's kind of love demands that we try. And this is the way that we, like God, can possibly play a healing role in their lives.

Let me emphasise once again that accepting people unconditionally does not mean "anything goes". If we want to follow God's example, we must stand against those things that break God's heart. This will mean making certain judgements between right and wrong, good and evil, truth and falsehood. For instance, it could be that where we work there is a dishonest business practice that we need to oppose. Or a situation of abuse that we need to expose. However, this does not mean that we have to condemn the persons involved. We can hate the sin and love the sinner.

We see this principle very clearly in the life of Nelson Mandela. He despised the system of apartheid and all that it did to human beings. He spent his life fighting it. Nonetheless, he could still reach out and accept as his neighbour those who were instruments of this evil policy. I think especially of his relationship with his prison guards, even going so far as to invite one of them to be present at his presidential inauguration. It was a wonderful gesture and showed his ability to accept people as they are, even when he radically disagreed with what they had done.

DO WHATEVER GOOD IS POSSIBLE

Unlike some of his followers today, Jesus would have had no problem with being called a "do-gooder". Indeed, it was one of the ways in which those who knew him well interpreted his actions. He was described as a man who "went around doing good".[3] There was nothing passive about Jesus' response to the sinful world. Whenever he could, he did whatever good was possible. This is how he reflected God's attitude, and how we can as well.

We can start right where we are. Opportunities abound for us to fill our everyday lives with as much doing-good as possible. We can stop lying and speak the truth. We can offer practical assistance to others in the seemingly trivial tasks of daily living. We can be courteous and kind. We can raise our voices against crime and corruption and other forms of violence. We can seek to relieve human suffering and need wherever we can. We can lend our support to those initiatives aimed at making our communities safer and better places in which to live. In all these ways, and there are many others as well, we can allow God's light to shine through us in our dark world.

IN A NUTSHELL

In our search for peace and serenity we must be careful not to distance ourselves from the human struggles that take place on the streets around us. Even if they unsettle the untroubled waters of our inner calm! When faced with evil, we can learn to reflect the attitude of God. God accepts us without any "ifs" or "buts". He discerns between the sinner and the sin. He desires that as much goodness as possible be injected into human life. As we follow his example in these ways, we take "this sinful world as it is and not as we would have it." If we are willing to try these things, it might even be that the headlines of our newspapers may one day look different.

What would it mean for you to reflect God's non-condemning attitude towards those around you?

For God did not send his Son

into the world to condemn

the world, but to save the

world through him.

JOHN 3:17

CHAPTER 9

TRUSTING THAT HE WILL MAKE
ALL THINGS RIGHT

"ALL THE KING'S HORSES, and all the king's men, couldn't put Humpty Dumpty together again." When our lives get broken we may sometimes feel like this. Yet the Bible has some wonderful promises for those who are trying to put their lives together again. For example, in the Old Testament, in the second chapter of the prophecy of Joel, God says,

I will restore the years that the locusts have eaten.[1]

Here God is not only offering to forgive us and allow us to start again with a clean slate, but is also promising to help us restore our broken and ruined lives to something of the usefulness and fullness they had before. Perhaps even more so. Circumstances might be very different for us now, but we can become whole and fruitful again with God's help.

Another magnificent promise comes from Paul in the eighth chapter of his letter to the Christians in Rome:

> ...we know that in all things God works for the good of those who love him...[2]

Think about these words for a few moments. God wants to take everything that has happened in our lives and use it for good, somewhere, sometime. Even the painful and bad things like the exam failure, the unwanted divorce, the collapse of a business, a struggle with addiction, the limitations of growing old, or a terrible sin. Every detail of our lives, offered to God, can be reworked into something beautiful. Isn't that incredible?

The Serenity Prayer challenges us to take promises like these seriously. It asks us to live each day, "trusting that God will make all things right".

But, as we all know, such trust is not easy to come by. We cannot make trust happen, or manufacture it, or work it up by repeatedly telling ourselves to "just trust – just have faith". There are strong forces both in and around our lives that work against us having a real confident trust in God.

In the end, we have to realise that genuine faith in God actually comes as a gift. Of course, when we grasp this truth, we must not fall into the error of believing there is nothing which we must do. There is something very important that we have to do. We need to place ourselves on the path of trusting. From our side, this is how we express our desire and our willingness to receive the gift. Here are three simple pointers as to how we can do this.

GET TO KNOW WHAT GOD IS REALLY LIKE

Our starting point in placing our lives on the path of trusting is to get to know what God is really like. Let me explain why. We will only entrust ourselves to God with confidence if we believe deep down that God is good and trustworthy. If we do not believe this, it is highly unlikely that we will commit ourselves wholeheartedly. We will remain cautious, defensive and untrusting. Can you see why our ideas about God are so important? They determine whether we relate trustingly to God or not.

So let me ask you to think about some of the ideas you may have about God. Here are some questions that may help you to clarify your present understanding.

- Do you believe God causes evil things to happen?
- When something bad happens to you, do you think that God is punishing you?

- Do you feel that God is out to get you if you put a foot out of line?
- Do you believe that God will love you less if you do something wrong?
- Do you believe that evil is more powerful than God?

If you have answered yes to any of these questions, it will probably be very difficult for you to pray the Serenity Prayer and really mean it. It is hard to really believe that things can be made right if we believe that God is fickle or vengeful or impotent. Yet this often is the distorted understanding of God that many people carry in their hearts and minds.

One of the best ways to correct our thinking about what God is really like is to try to see God through the eyes of Jesus. Jesus shows us that God is our Heavenly Parent who never gives up loving us, no matter how much we mess up. He teaches us that this is God's world and that God treasures every part of it, including you and me. He reminds us that, although we live in the midst of incredible pain, suffering and evil, God will have the final word. These are just some of the truths that Jesus brings into our hearts. As we interact with them, we see that God can be trusted and our faith gradually begins to deepen.

SPEND TIME WITH OTHER TRUSTERS

Another way to place our lives on the path of trusting is to spend time with other trusters. Almost daily we come across people whose faithful and believing lives help us to trust more. By giving us real-life glimpses of trust, they take trusting out of the realm of abstract theory and give it flesh and blood. Here are some of the trusters that I have known. All of them are people who, even in the midst of difficulty and heartache, have kept trust alive. They encourage me more than they will ever know. I hope that they will encourage you too.

A bereaved husband sings the hymn "O Love that wilt not let me go" with tear-filled eyes at the memorial service for his young wife who has died of cancer.

A recovering alcoholic picks himself up after a relapse that resulted in the loss of his job and commits himself once again to staying sober one day at a time.

A middle-aged executive, because of his faith, refuses to back down on a moral issue, even though his principles may block future advancement in the company where he works.

A couple describe how, at the end of each day, they cup their hands, raise them upwards and symbolically release both their children into the hands of God.

A dear friend continues in weekly worship, daily prayer and a life of sacrificial servanthood amongst the poorest of the poor, in spite of being tormented by doubts about the goodness of God that have been raised by the context in which he works.

A frail elderly man, still grieving for his wife who passed away seven years ago, and who now lives alone in a nearby retirement home, kneels down at the side of his bed each day and thanks God for all the blessings he has received.

When we spend time with people like this, and others like them, we discover that trust engenders trust. This has happened for me so many times over the past years. When we try to go it alone along the spiritual path, it is very easy for the flame of faith to start to flicker, and sometimes even go out. This is when we need to spend time with those who have gone through dark valleys and yet have kept trusting. Somehow their presence fans to life the struggling flames of our faith and helps us to trust more deeply that God will make all things right.

PUT TO WORK WHATEVER FAITH WE DO HAVE

A third way we place our lives on the path of trusting involves putting to work whatever faith we do have, even if it is as small as a mustard seed. When we act on the little faith we do have, we find that our trust begins to grow, generating a wider and deeper belief in God's goodness, love and competence. Here are a few suggestions of ways in which we can activate our faith and help our trust in God to become stronger.

- We can talk to God on a daily basis about the things that are worrying us and causing us anxiety. When we experience God helping us in these situations, our trust in God deepens.
- We can meditate regularly on some of the ideas that Jesus gives us about God. For example, we can take the idea that we are unconditionally loved by God and dwell on it for a few weeks, or even months. Over time we discover that the truth has sunk deep into our hearts and become a real part of our lives.

- We can notice the goodness of God in all the things we enjoy, and give thanks for them. All of them are hints of God's love and care for us. When we praise God for them, God becomes more real in our experience and our faith grows.

- We can intentionally work at growing our relationship with God by attending worship, receiving communion, joining a small group, reading the Bible and taking time out of the busyness of the day to be alone with God. Even when we do these things without strong feelings of faith, God has a way of growing our faith as we do them.

- We can risk doing something for others that we sense God wants us to do. It may perhaps be getting alongside someone who is going through a hard time, or sharing some of our material resources with those in need, or telling someone about what God means to us. When we experience God using these small efforts, often in ways that go beyond our wildest dreams, our faith matures.

The Serenity Prayer reminds us that, if we are going to find a deep inner peace, we need to trust God to make all things right. Holding on to this belief in the midst of hardship and heartache can be extremely difficult. However, when we get to know what God is really like, spend time with other trusters and put whatever faith we do have to work, our trust in God will grow and grow. As this happens, we will discover in our own experience that trusting God and finding serenity are always inseparable companions.

How would you describe your present level of trust and faith in God?

And we know that in all

things God works for the

good of those who love

him, who have been called

according to his purpose.

ROMANS 8:28

CHAPTER 10

IF I SURRENDER TO HIS WILL

A T THE RISK OF OVER-SIMPLIFYING THINGS, there seem to be two groups of people in our world. On the one hand, there are some whose hearts and minds are turned away from God, and have little interest in what God wants for them. They want to be their own bosses. Their lives are focused on themselves, their own needs, and what they want to do. Their theme song might well be Frank Sinatra singing "I'll do it my way".

On the other hand, there are people whose lives are directed towards God. Although they sometimes experience moods and feelings that want to pull them in other directions, what matters most for them is finding and doing God's will. Deep down they want to let God be God in their lives. It could be said that the prayer written across their hearts is, "not my will, but yours be done". Since you are reading this chapter it is probable that you are closer to this second group of people.

While the power and energy of God's love is constantly

reaching out to touch all of us, it is those in the second group who receive the gift of God's peace. We can know this from reflecting on our own experience. When we seek and do God's will, we usually feel an increase of inner tranquillity, contentment and joy. Even though this sometimes involves tough choices, or going against the crowd, when we do what our conscience tells us to do, our hearts and minds are marked by a deep inner calm. Perhaps it is for this reason that the Serenity Prayer assumes a willingness on our part to surrender ourselves to the will of God for our lives.

GOD'S GENERAL WILL

But what do we actually mean when we talk about "the will of God"? Is it some kind of fixed, heavenly blueprint? Something God has already mapped out for our lives? Or is it something that we work out together with God and with each other? Is our only choice in the matter whether we fit in or don't fit in with what God has already planned? Or is there room in all this for our personal initiative and decision-making? Indeed, what does it mean to surrender ourselves to God's will, as the Serenity Prayer asks us to do?

A helpful picture drawn from my own experience as a parent may throw some light on these questions. When my children were little, they would often play together in the back yard. My general will for them was fairly straightforward. I wanted them to know that I was nearby if they needed me, to enjoy themselves, to get along with each other, and not hurt themselves. For the rest, they were entirely free to choose whatever games they wanted to play, how they wanted to divide their time between the different activities, what toys they played with and even whether they came indoors or not. In these matters I did not want to control them or impose my will on them.

The general will of God operates in a similar way. Generally speaking, we could say that God wants us to live fulfilled, loving and honest lives. Although the Bible gives lots of guidance about what this may involve, we can be sure that God also allows us plenty of scope for personal initiative and decision-making. Indeed, there can be little doubt that God wants us to play a large part in determining our own path through life. Let me illustrate this balance between God's will and our freedom by exploring with you three aspects of God's overall plan for our lives.

DEVELOP AND USE OUR GIFTS

Each one of us has been created with and given certain gifts. These have been placed in us by our Creator God and they represent our unrepeatable uniqueness. God's general will for our lives is intimately linked with this giftedness. Indeed, there is an important sense in which we can say that the general will of God for our lives is written into the very fabric of who we are. Our surrender to God's will then becomes, to a large extent, surrender to these gifts. At the very least, this means finding out what they are, developing them as best we can, and then putting them to creative use. As a poster once proclaimed,

> Who we are is God's gift to us,
> Who we become is our gift to God.

BECOME A LOVING PERSON

There is also no doubt that God wants each one of us to become a more loving person. In the Bible we are told that because God is love, when we take up residence in a life of love, we live in God and God lives in us.[1] We deliberately choose to live in this house of love when we take small steps to care and show concern every time there is an opportunity. This may simply mean greeting someone warmly, listening attentively, making a phone call, sending an SMS, popping in for a visit, preparing a meal, buying a gift, giving a hug, making a financial contribution, offering a helping hand. All these small actions express love to people around us and this is a crucial part of God's general will for our lives.

Furthermore, not only does the Bible tell us that God is love, it is also at pains to tell us that God is light.[2] And it goes on to say that we need to walk in the light if we really want to experience God fully. This does not mean that we have to be perfect, but it does mean that we must be willing to be honest, to take off our masks, to be open and transparent in our relationships, to admit our failings and faults, and above all, to stop lying and speak the truth. Becoming this kind of person, and living this kind of life, puts us at the very heart of God's general will.

It is very important for us to be clear that these three aspects of God's general will do not rule out personal choices. We still have to decide for ourselves how we intend to develop and use our gifts, or what the most loving thing will be in a certain situation, or how we will walk in the light. As we make these kinds of decisions, we can certainly ask God for wisdom along the lines of what was suggested in Chapter 4. It often happens that God will give us special insights and promptings, but in the end we ourselves still have to take responsibility for our choices and actions.

So far we have been thinking about God's general will. He also has a specific will for our lives. Let me take the picture I used earlier one step further. While I have a general will for my children most of the time, there are moments when I have something very specific in mind for each of them to do. When this is the case I usually ask them to do a task which is quite definite and precise. No one else can do it for me except the child I have asked. My request could be understood as a special assignment that I have entrusted to him or her.

In the same way, there are times when our Heavenly Parent has something very specific in mind for each one of us to do. A very old Christian tradition celebrates this truth when it states that God sends each person into the world with a special message to deliver, a special song to sing, and a special act of love to bestow. No one else can convey my message, sing my song, or do my act of love. These are entrusted to me alone. Mother Teresa once said, "Each one of us has something beautiful to do for God."

How do we go about uncovering God's specific will for our lives? As we all know, it is not usually written across the sky in bold letters! Nor do we receive a computer print-out. Most times we have to try and discern what this personal calling will be in our lives. Because it usually changes with the different seasons of our lives, this quest to discover God's personal call is an on-going process. Here are a few pointers which I hope will help you find out what it is that God has in mind for you.

- Finding God's specific will assumes that we have a living relationship with God. We cannot manufacture or generate our own calls. They are discovered and discerned in the context of an ever-deepening intimacy with God. All of us, if we really want to discover our personal calling, need to take seriously the second to last step in the twelve-step recovery programme from Alcoholics Anonymous. It reads: "Sought through prayer and meditation to improve our conscious contact with God, praying only for knowledge of his will for us and the power to carry it out."

- Finding God's specific will nourishes our lives. We must always remember that the God who calls us is the God who loves us and wants us to be fully alive. We can therefore be sure that when we are doing what God wants us to do, it will bring with it a deep sense of fulfilment and joy. It also follows that one of the best things we can do to discern our personal calling is to sit down and make a list of all those things that give us life.

- Finding God's specific will also enriches the lives of people around us. It has a strange way of pointing our hearts and minds towards our neighbour, connecting our giftedness with some segment of the world's pain, and meeting real human need. In the words of St Francis, when we follow God's call, we become instruments of God's peace, bringing love where there is hatred, pardon where there is injury, faith where there is doubt, light where there is darkness.

- Finding God's specific will also means that we often have to deal with deep feelings of resistance. Like Moses in the Bible, when God calls us we will often duck and dive. Some of our favourite excuses will probably be the very ones that Moses himself used. You might recognise them. "I don't matter", "I don't know enough about God", "What happens if I fail?", "I don't have what it takes", "Someone else can do it better".

IN A NUTSHELL

If we want to receive the gift of God's peace, we must find and do God's will which has two dimensions. There is God's general will for us to live our lives as fully, lovingly and honestly as possible. This will involve using and developing our gifts, giving love priority, and walking in the light. And there is also God's specific will. This is our personal calling which we discover as we grow in relationship with God, pay attention to what nourishes our lives and those of others, and deal with our resistance. When we surrender ourselves to both these dimensions of God's will, our lives will be marked by a new, hitherto unknown serenity.

What do you sense is God's specific
will for your life?

Yet not as I will, but as you will.

MATTHEW 26:39

CHAPTER 11

THAT I MAY BE REASONABLY HAPPY IN THIS LIFE

*H*OW HAPPY ARE YOU? This is probably one of the most important questions that we can ever ask ourselves and one another. The pursuit of happiness is universal. Through the ages great spiritual thinkers have always maintained that God created us to be happy. This could be why the desire for happiness runs so deeply in all of our hearts. Most of us, when asked what we want most from life, will usually respond with something like, "I just want to be happy."

However, it doesn't take a scientist to see that there are not too many happy people around. Casual observation shows us this. Look, for a moment, at the soaring divorce figures, the increased incidence of suicide, the frequent occurrences of road rage, the growing dependencies on tranquillisers and the spiralling statistics of domestic violence. It is not surprising that the medical journals tell us that depression is one of the most widespread diseases of the modern era. It seems that we are living in a world where unhappiness is the norm and true happiness is the exception.

SO LET ME ASK AGAIN: "HOW HAPPY ARE YOU?"

By happiness I mean a deep sense of inner well-being and contentment, the experience of being fully alive; alive to ourselves, to others and to God. As we shall see, happiness actually has very little to do with external circumstances and events. In this respect, it is significantly different from the experience of pleasure which is far more tied to circumstances and dependent on "feel-good" factors. So to help you respond to the above question, here is a quick homemade quiz. If you answer "true" to the majority of the following statements, it is probable that happiness has become a stranger in your life. This chapter, then, may well have been written especially for you.

- I seldom enjoy the good things of life.
- I have lost a lot of my motivation for doing things.
- I live with a constant sense of discontent and dissatisfaction.
- I struggle to accept myself and often compare myself negatively with others.

- I tend to blame others for the difficult situations I find myself in.
- I seldom look for and find the good in myself, others and the situations of my life.
- I fear closeness and intimacy and rarely communicate deeply with others.
- I have little sense that I am using my God-given gifts and talents to the best of my ability.
- I feel constantly guilty and bad about myself.
- I have little connection with God.

REASONABLY HAPPY

Perhaps one of the greatest mistakes we make in our search for happiness is our insistence on being happy at all costs, at all times. I was made aware of this again recently. I was interviewing an attractive young lady in her early twenties who had struggled for a number of years with suicidal thoughts and dark depression. With the support of her family, a caring psychiatrist and friends from her local congregation, she was gradually finding new ways to approach life. When I asked her for the secret of her recovery, she answered, "I've learned how unrealistic it is to expect to be completely happy all the time."

This is exactly the secret of the Serenity Prayer. When we

realise that we cannot always be happy, it encourages us to pray that we may be "reasonably happy in this life". There are often times when we have to do not-so-happy things. Things like speaking the truth in a difficult situation, or admitting that we were in the wrong, or facing a painful relationship issue, or confronting a colleague on an ethical issue, or going to the dentist! In these situations we put our desire for happiness on hold in order to do what needs to be done, even if we don't feel like doing it and it causes us inner discomfort.

Quite frankly, it is also a huge relief when we can accept that we don't have to try to be happy all the time. The fact is that there are moments when cheerfulness is simply not appropriate. One thinks especially of when we are going through a dark period of painful grief and loss. This is a time not so much for laughter and joy, but for tears and sadness. Few things are more cruel when you are mourning than to have someone come along with a bright and cheery smile, slap you on your back, give you a glib religious platitude and tell you to be happy. Certainly, that is not what the Serenity Prayer is all about.

HAPPINESS BEGINS ON THE INSIDE

Happiness, like serenity, originates inside ourselves. Too often we depend on outside things, and even other people, to make us happy. We think to ourselves that if only we could get a better joy, or meet the right partner, or win the Lotto, we will find the happiness that we are missing. It seldom, if ever, works like that. To be sure, external factors do affect our lives for better or for worse, but to find an enduring happiness we need to take a much closer look at what happens inside us. This sets the tone for the way we respond to what happens around us.

It has taken me years to learn this. Like you, my life has the usual roller coaster ups and downs. Sometimes things go well. At other times they go badly. It could be that the washing machine starts leaking, the dog gets sick, the car breaks down, the unit trusts drop in interest – sometimes all at once! Blaming these outside circumstances for how I am feeling seldom leads me towards happiness. I need to look within myself and assume responsibility for how I respond. Recently I read a book where the author reminds himself of this each day.[1] Over his bathroom mirror he has put a sign which he sees and reads each morning:

YOU ARE LOOKING AT THE FACE OF THE PERSON WHO IS RESPONSIBLE FOR YOUR HAPPINESS.

The most important place to begin taking this responsibility is in the area of our feelings. Often we get ambushed by feelings and emotions that destroy our happiness. If we are going to be reasonably happy in this life, we need to deal with these feelings as creatively and responsibly as possible. Rather than being overwhelmed by them, or pretending they are not there, we need to identify and name them: "This is what I am feeling at the moment – anger, hostility, envy, boredom." Then we need to share these feelings with God and ask God to show us how best to live with them. When we are able to channel the energy within our feelings into creative action, we live far happier lives. But we need to do this ourselves. No one can do it for us.

HAPPINESS IS A BY-PRODUCT

There is a verse which says:

> Happiness is a butterfly.
> The more you chase it, the more it will elude you.
> But if you turn your attention to other things,
> It comes and sits softly on your shoulder.

These words have something very important to teach us. They remind us that if we try to pursue happiness as an end in itself, we will usually miss it. When we make it our "god", and spend our lives searching for it, we end up chasing rainbows. Neither does it just fall into our lives by sheer chance. True happiness comes as a gift from God, a freely given by-product of a particular way of life that comes to us when we stop feverishly seeking it.

All this goes against the grain of our consumer culture. Every day, especially through the advertising world, we are bombarded with messages which tell us that happiness is a marketable commodity which can be bought. If we buy the "right car", or use the "right deodorant", or go on the "right holiday", we will be happy. Happiness, in other words, becomes a shopping list. If the advertisers are to be believed, our being happy depends entirely on having what they consider to be indispensable. It is one of the great deceptions of our time.

The Serenity Prayer stands in stark contrast to this. It locates our desire for happiness against the larger background of our relationship with God. Did you notice that the line about "being reasonably happy" follows immediately after the ones that speak of "trusting that he will make all things right" and "if I surrender to his will". This sequence is not accidental. It suggests that the more we are able to trust that God can bring good out of evil, and the more we are able to surrender ourselves to God's purposes, the happier we will be. Giving our primary attention to things like faith and obedience allows the butterfly of happiness to come and sit on our shoulder.

IN A NUTSHELL

We can only make our world a happier place if we ourselves first learn to be happy in our own hearts. We set out on this learning journey when we develop reasonable expectations with regard to happiness, start to take responsibility for the way we respond to life, and allow God to really be God in our lives. This is the recipe that the Serenity Prayer offers us in our quest for happiness. And happy is the person who follows this wisdom.

How happy are you?

THAT I MAY BE REASONABLY HAPPY IN THIS LIFE

The joy of the Lord is your strength.

NEHEMIAH 8:10

CHAPTER 12

AND SUPREMELY HAPPY
WITH HIM FOREVER

YEARS AGO WHEN I TAUGHT confirmation classes, I would ask the young people whether they thought heaven was a wonderful place. Almost always they would all respond positively. I would then follow up with another question. Who amongst them, if they could choose, would decide to go to heaven immediately? No one ever raised their hands. All of them preferred to delay the pleasure!

Let me quickly say that, when it comes to the second question, I hesitate as well. A huge part of me really loves and enjoys this world, difficult and evil as it often is, and wants to postpone my departure from it for as long as I can. Besides I don't like thinking too much about death and dying, either my own or the death of those close to me. Nonetheless, as I get older, I am finding myself thinking more and more about heaven. And even though I don't want to go there just yet, the hope of heaven has become very important to me.

117

What are your thoughts and feelings about heaven? Here are some simple questions which can help you clarify your thinking.

- How do you feel about your own death?
- What are your dominant thoughts and feelings at a funeral?
- What images come to mind when the word "heaven" is mentioned?
- Is heaven the kind of place where you would like to spend eternity?
- Do you think you would get bored with being in heaven?

We don't always find it easy to think more deeply about these things. However, honestly working through questions like these puts us in touch with what we really think and feel about death and dying. Furthermore, they help us to evaluate critically our thoughts and feelings in the light of the three ideas offered by the Serenity Prayer on the subject.

SUPREMELY HAPPY

First of all, the Serenity Prayer suggests that in heaven we will be "supremely happy". We will no longer be frustrated by our shortcomings and limitations, or by our failures in loving and forgiving, or by the gap between who we are and who we long to be. In heaven we will be utterly fulfilled and satisfied, in our loving and our knowing, our working and playing, our resting and worshipping. Dare we allow ourselves to imagine what this may be like? Here is one way we can try.

Think of a moment in your life when you were really happy. It could have been a time of deep intimacy with someone special, or the birth of your child, or a special birthday party, or the completion of a difficult task or the joy of your wedding day. Whatever it was, multiply this experience of happiness many times. This is just a little of what we will experience when we live together with God in heaven. As one writer so beautifully puts it, "Maybe the happiest memories of ourselves on earth are our clearest images of what we shall be like in heaven."[1]

This is the hope celebrated by the Serenity Prayer. In heaven we will know a depth of happiness that we have never known before. Whatever we spend eternity doing, and there are some wonderful clues in the Bible about what this may involve, we will be deeply joyful, sharing in that supreme happiness which God enjoys all the time. We will hear the words, spoken by Jesus in one of his parables, "Come and share your Master's happiness."[2]

The second thing the Serenity Prayer teaches us about our life in heaven is that we will be supremely happy "with him". We will not be in isolation. We will be with God. The glimpses which have come to us in this life through faith will be replaced by clear vision. We will meet God, as it were, face to face.

There is a delightful story about twins, talking to each other in the womb, which illustrates this hope. As they snuggle up against each other, the sister suddenly turns to her brother and says, "I believe there is life after birth."

"Nonsense," answers her brother, "this dark and warm place is all there is."

"There must be something more than this confined space," insists the baby girl. "There must be somewhere where there is light and vision and freedom to move."

Her twin brother is still not convinced. After a few moments of silence, she goes on hesitantly, "There is something else, and I'm afraid you won't believe that either, but I think there is a mother!"

"A mother!" shouts her brother furiously. "What are you talking about? I have never seen a mother and neither have you. Who put that crazy idea in your head? This place is all we have. Why do you want more? It's good to be here. We have all we need, so let's be content."

The sister is quite shocked by her brother's anger and doesn't say any more. However, she cannot ignore her instincts, and since there is no one to speak to except her twin brother, she finally plucks up courage to ask him, "Do you sometimes feel those unpleasant and painful squeezes that come every once in a while?"

"Yes," he answers. "What's so special about that?"

"Well," explains his sister, "I think those squeezes are getting us ready for that other place which is far more beautiful and spacious than this, where we will see our mother face to face."

FOREVER

The third idea that the Serenity Prayer gives about our life in heaven is that we will be supremely happy with God "forever". Unlike candles in the wind, the light of our lives will never be extinguished. Although we can be sure that the moment of physical death will bring about many significant changes, our personal existence will somehow continue without interruption. We are not going to disappear into an eternal mist, or be kept in some parking place for the dead, or waft around in an angelic haze. God loves us too much for this to happen and will keep us safe eternally.

Another way of putting this idea, in the words of a dear friend, is to understand ourselves as unceasing spiritual beings with an eternal destiny in God's universe.[3] Take time, if you will, to commit this mind-boggling sentence to memory. This is who we are. We are not just our brains, any more than we are our spleens, or lungs, or blood. Even though our bodies are essential for our lives in this world, we are far more than our bodies. Rather, as Jesus makes clear in different parts of the Gospels, we are embodied spirits, created out of love, of more value to God than all the rest of creation put together, who are never going to see death.

If we do possess an eternal future,[4] as suggested above, it would be extremely wise to prepare for it. Since we are essentially spiritual beings, this preparation must include a real, genuine and growing relationship with God. So let us be reminded for one last time of what was affirmed in the first chapter of this book:

There is a God. This God is totally good, totally loving and totally competent. He has come to us in Jesus Christ, whom we can totally trust.

There is no better way to aim for heaven, than to arrange our lives around this breathtaking news. My hope and prayer is that the previous meditations on the various thoughts of the Serenity Prayer will help us to begin to do this. We will discover, as C.S. Lewis once said, that when we aim for heaven, earth is thrown in as well.

IN A NUTSHELL

Our ideas about death and what comes after our dying are critical. They affect our lives in this world more than we fully realise. The Serenity Prayer offers three important thoughts about what our live in heaven will be like. It will be a new dimension where our lives overflow with joy; where we will at last behold the loving face of our Creator God and where our lives will never cease to be. When we build these three ideas into our belief system, and allow them to transform the way we live, we will find ourselves well on the way to a serene, peaceful and deeply meaningful life.

What are your feelings about dying and the afterlife?

I am the resurrection and the life. He

who believes in me will live, even

though he dies; and whoever lives and

believes in me will never die.

JOHN 11:25–26

NOTES

Chapter 1 God grant me the serenity

1. "Peace I leave with you…" (John 14:27).
2. I am in debt to Dallas Willard for this helpful summary of the biblical message.

Chapter 3 Courage to change the things I can

1. The illustration of the escalator comes from Keith Miller's book *A Hunger For Healing* (New York: Harper Collins, 1991).

Chapter 4 Wisdom to know the difference

1. "If any of you is lacking in wisdom…" (James 1:5, NRSV).

Chapter 5 Living one day at a time

1. I learnt this way of doing a nightly review from Dennis Linn, Sheila Frabicant Linn and Matthew Linn in their book, *Sleeping With Bread* (New York: Paulist Press, 1994).

Chapter 6 Enjoying one moment at a time

1. "…anyone who will not receive the kingdom of God like a little child will never enter it" (Luke 18:17).
2. "The thief comes only to steal and kill and destroy…" (John 10:10).

Chapter 7 Accepting hardships as the pathway to peace

1. "There is…one God and Father of all, who is over all and through all and in all" (Ephesians 4:6).

Chapter 8 Taking, as he did, the sinful world as it is, not as I would have it

1. "For God did not send his Son into the world to condemn the world, but to save the world through him" (John 3:17).
2. "Do not judge, or you too will be judged" (Matthew 7:1).
3. "…he went around doing good…" (Acts 10:38).

Chapter 9 Trusting that he will make all things right

1. "I will restore the years that the locusts have eaten" (Joel 2:25).
2. "And we know that in all things God works for the good of those who love him…" (Romans 8:28).
3. "Anyone who has seen me has seen the Father" (John 14:9).

Chapter 10 If I surrender to his will

1. "God is love. Whoever lives in love lives in God, and God in him" (1 John 4:16).
2. "God is light…" (1 John 1:5).

Chapter 11 That I may be reasonably happy in this life

1. The author to whom I refer is John Powell who wrote *Happiness Is An Inside Job* (Valencia: Tabor, 1989).

Chapter 12 And supremely happy with him forever

1. This wonderful sentence about heaven comes from Lewis Smede's book *Keeping Hope Alive* (Nashville: Thomas Nelson, 1998).
2. "Come and share your Master's happiness" (Matthew 25:21).
3. My philosopher friend is Dallas Willard. He develops this concept about the spiritual dimension of human life in *Divine Conspiracy* (New York: Harper Collins, 1998).
4. Jesus' views about our unceasing existence can be traced in verses like Matthew 10:28, John 8:51–52 and John 11:26.

THE STORY BEHIND
THE SERENITY PRAYER

In order to get the background of the Serenity Prayer, I used the following resources:

Sobriety and Beyond by Father John Doe (Indianapolis: SMT Guild, Inc., 1995).

Pass It On (New York: Alcoholics Anonymous World Services, Inc., 1984).

Sobriety Without End by Father John Doe (Indianapolis: SMT Guild, Inc., 1957).

The AA Experience by Milton A. Maxwell (New York: McGraw Hill Book Company, 1984).

Alcoholics Anonymous Comes of Age (New York: Alcoholics Anonymous World Services, Inc., 1957).

Reflections on the Serenity Prayer by Philip St Romain (Liguori: Liguori Publications, 1997).